Extraordinary Clouds

Skies of the unexpected from the beautiful to the bizarre

Extraordinary Clouds

Skies of the unexpected from the beautiful to the bizarre

Richard Hamblyn

David and Charles

In association with the

With thanks to the Cloud Appreciation Society

A DAVID & CHARLES BOOK
Copyright © David & Charles Limited 2009

David & Charles is an F+W Media Inc. company
4700 East Galbraith Road
Cincinnati, OH 45236

First published in the UK in 2009
First published in the US in 2009

Text copyright © Richard Hamblyn 2009
Photographs copyright © the copyright holders (see page 142)

A catalogue record for this book is available from the British Library.

ISBN-13: 978-07153-3281-8 paperback
ISBN-10: 0-7153-3281-3 paperback

Printed in China by SNP Leefung
for David & Charles
Brunel House, Newton Abbot, Devon

Commissioning Editor: Neil Baber
Editorial Manager: Emily Pitcher
Editor: Verity Muir
Senior Designer: Jodie Lystor
Production Controller: Beverley Richardson

Visit our website at www.davidandcharles.co.uk

David & Charles books are available from all good bookshops; alternatively
you can contact our Orderline on 0870 9908222 or write to us at FREEPOST
EX2 110, D&C Direct, Newton Abbot, TQ12 4ZZ (no stamp required UK only);
US customers call 800-289-0963 and Canadian customers call 800-840-5220.

CONTENTS

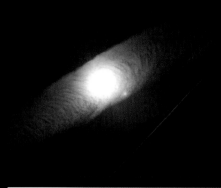

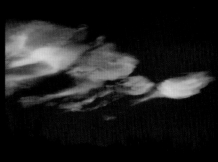

Foreword

Clouds are one of the most photographed natural phenomena and have long inspired me to learn more about our planet's atmosphere.

Over the years I've looked skywards with a mixture of excitement and awe at different cloud formations, including in the South Atlantic, the Tropics and the mountainous regions of the world. This book contains some wonderfully vivid examples of the clouds that can be seen from these vantage points.

Air travel affords the keen observer a tantalizing, yet fleeting, glimpse of clouds from above. As this book shows the advent of satellite technology has added a stunning new dimension that allows us to look down on clouds in glorious detail. In my job as Operations Director at the Met Office, I use animated images from satellites to understand how weather systems and clouds evolve and change.

All this activity overhead suggests that there's more to feeling 'under the weather' than most people realize. The cumulus and cirrus of a bright summer's day can give us a real emotional lift, while the stratus of a grey winter's day can dull our spirits and leave us longing for the sun. I still get a tingle of excitement at the sight of a developing cumulonimbus or the chaotic sky of altocumulus, while feeling the air heavy with the prospect of a thunderstorm.

To me, all clouds are extraordinary as they're a visible indication of the planet's fascinating atmosphere at work. Behind the camera my skill is very limited so I have great admiration for the photographers who have captured the spectacular images in this book. For every picture I try to visualize the weather pattern that gave rise to the conditions – from the benign to the extreme.

I hope you get as much pleasure from them as I do.

Keith Groves
Met Office Operations Director

Introduction

'A cloud is nothing else but a great heap of snow close clinging together', the philosopher René Descartes declared in 1637, and in a strictly material sense he was right: most clouds consist of ice crystals and supercooled water droplets that have condensed around billions of tiny nuclei present in the atmosphere between 1 and 10 kilometres (3,280 and 32,800ft) above the Earth's surface. They form through a variety of physical processes and have varying life-spans ranging from a few seconds or minutes (in the case of some of the man-made clouds) to many hours or even days (in the case of some of the stratiform varieties created by the lifting of extensive layers of moisture-laden air).

But there is more to clouds than the bare facts of their material and physical circumstances, at least from our earthbound human perspective. They also present us with an ongoing visual spectacle that transforms the sky into a constantly changing, mood-altering display of light, shade, volume and colour – 'the ultimate art gallery above', as nature writer Ralph Waldo Emerson described it. A vast outdoor exhibition space that is open to everyone – even in those places unfortunate enough to suffer blue skies all year round such as carefree California, which not only boasts America's emptiest skies but also the highest number of people in therapy. How depressing it must be to never see a stratocumulus, or to have to wait a month or more for a glimpse of a simple cumulus mediocris, let alone a display of galloping cirrus (see page 53). As the Athenian playwright Aristophanes pointed out in the early 5th century BCE, clouds are 'the patron goddesses of idle men, and it is from them that we derive our intelligence, our conversation and our reason' – the very qualities that make civilization possible. Life without clouds would not only be physically unendurable – apart from their rain-bearing function they act as a finely-tuned planetary thermostat – it would also deprive us of one of the principal agents of creative contemplation, those mutable, gregarious, life-affirming thought-bubbles that drift continuously overhead.

This book is devoted to showcasing some of the world's most unusual and arresting cloud phenomena, ranging from small-scale optical ephemera such as coronae and haloes, to the big-budget summer spectaculars of hurricanes and tornadoes which, despite their wanton destructiveness, offer magnificent views of the atmosphere operating at full capacity. The image of Hurricane Katrina's eyewall on page 32 for instance takes us inside one of the most powerful structures on Earth, its coils of cloud contorting around the central vortex at speeds of over 250kph (150mph), while the photograph of the birth of a tornado on page 102 catches the moment that a supercell thunderstorm becomes fully tornadic, a cloud of dust and debris hurtling upwards as the mesocyclone hits the ground.

Though there is a fair amount of such *Sturm und Drang* (the conventional translation is storm and stress') excitement to be found in the following pages, some of my favourites are among the quieter scenes, such as the fragmentary ribbon of iridescent altocumulus on page 80, or the silent roll of advection fog advancing across the Australian desert at dawn shown on page 13. Both these images were taken by members of the Cloud Appreciation Society (CAS) – as are nearly a quarter of the photographs in this book. CAS is an online community of cloud enthusiasts, founded by Gavin Pretor-Pinney in the summer of 2004 in order (as its founder put it) 'to fight the banality of blue-sky thinking'. With a worldwide membership of over 13,000 and an ever-expanding archive of cloud photographs (the collection currently stands at more that 4,500 images, with new photographs added every week), the Society has become an important resource for cloud researchers all over the world. The willingness of its members to donate their often unique pictures to the archive, free of charge, is a testament to the benevolence that clouds inspire in their beholders. Take the image on page 73 for example, which shows the unusual sight of a fallstreak hole illuminated by the prismatic brightness of a circumzenithal arc. It was taken by the Cambridge-based photographer John Deed who came across the sight by chance while taking his son to football practice one cold September morning: 'While he was warming up to play I went for a short walk. When I looked up above me there was this large tongue-shaped hole in the cloud. This was interesting in itself but then I realized that there was a rainbow at one end or, as I now know, a circumzenithal arc (CZA). And as I looked closer there was a second one further down, although it does not show up on the picture very well.' A few days later, this rare – possibly unique – capture of a fallstreak hole with a double CZA is donated to the CAS's photo-archive, and something entirely new was added to the global repertoire of clouds.

Of course a question that came up more than once during the making of this book was: how reliable are these images in terms of their photographic integrity? From the outset my selection criteria ruled out any photograph that had been manipulated or enhanced, such processes serving only to diminish a picture's meteorological value (after all, this is a collection of extraordinary clouds, not extraordinary retouching techniques). Great pains have been taken to establish the credentials of every image in the book and I can confidently state that none of the following clouds is of the 'cumulus photoshoppus' variety – not even the strange rippling silver sky over Cedar Rapids, Iowa, that features on pages 90–91. It may look like something from a science fiction B movie but the photograph is entirely authentic – in fact dozens of similar pictures were taken of the same event which, along with footage from a local television news report, can be viewed on Iowa's KCRG-TV9 website, under the heading: 'What Were Those Clouds?', a question that could well have served as a fitting title for this book.

Whether viewed from a great distance – as with some of the satellite images featured in chapter one – or looming a little too close for comfort – like some of the breathtaking tornado pictures that appear in chapter four – clouds always repay our attention, for there is never a moment when nothing can be said to be happening to them. Always changing, always on the move, they are nature's most dynamic structures, revealing the otherwise invisible processes of our turbulent atmosphere. Even the most uncharismatic cloud (sorry nimbostratus, but you do have a habit of outstaying your welcome) has something to tell us about planetary conditions, but it is the unusual clouds – those skies of the unexpected – that command our attention, letting us know when something out of the ordinary is happening. And that is what this book is about: a celebration of things that are out of the ordinary, from the merest wisp of a fleeting dust devil to vast fields of thunderheads visible from space. Welcome to the world of extraordinary clouds.

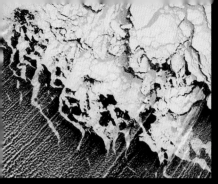
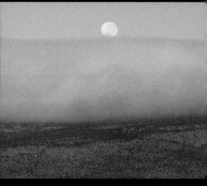
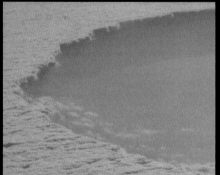

Clouds from the Air

Whether seen from a mountain summit, an aeroplane window or an orbiting satellite on the fringes of space, our atmosphere can exhibit some surprising characteristics when viewed from above.

An ocean of cloud

A creeping blanket of advection fog insinuates itself across the Severn Valley in Gloucestershire, England. A form of ground-level stratus cloud, advection fog is typically formed when mild, moist air hugs coastal inlets. Its vapour condenses into mist and fog when it passes over a cold surface – in this case a wide stretch of the River Severn, obscured from view at the top of the picture. Visibility on the ground was likely to have been less than a few hundred metres (about a thousand feet), although the official definition of fog is a visibility of less than 1 kilometre (c.1,600ft) – anything over that counts as mist. At the bottom left of the image the fog-waves break against the Cotswold escarpment, the eastern perimeter of the Severn Valley. The Domesday village of Nympsfield, on the path of a former Roman road, can be seen in the centre of the image.

Outback roll cloud

A roll of advection fog advances across the golden outback of Mount Augustus National Park, Western Australia. The phenomenon is formed by the same process described in the previous entry: a parcel of warm, moist air moving over the cold expanse of the early morning desert, condensing into ground-level stratus as the air is cooled to its dew point.

Photographer Sandy Boulter describes this dawn apparition as 'blue sky, moon and mist'. She took the photograph from the summit of Mount Augustus (or Burringurrah, as is it known by the Wadjari Aboriginal people), an 860m (2,820ft) sandstone formation that contends with the better-known Uluru (Ayers Rock) for the title of the world's largest monolith.

Edge of the cloudbank

An impressive view of the edge of an extensive bank of stratocumulus cloud draped like a blanket over the Mediterranean Sea. Stratocumulus are among the most common clouds on Earth, being routinely visible over large tracts of land and sea, though they can take a number of different forms and structures. The flat, extensive variety seen here is stratocumulus stratiformis which – as its name implies – has formed from the lifting or breaking up of sheets of low stratus cloud by means of upward convection. These rising sheets then thicken and merge to form a continuous layer of dense grey cloud, the curving edge of which marks the visible boundary of a slowly advancing cold front.

Wave clouds over the southern Indian Ocean

Amsterdam Island, one of the remotest islands on Earth, is a tiny volcanic peak rising from the faultline that separates the Antarctic from the Indo-Australian tectonic plates. Though only 881m (2,900ft) high, the island can affect the disposition of low cloud over the southern Indian Ocean. A layer of humid air rising and falling as it passes over the island has formed a sequence of narrow lenticular clouds that ride on the crests of these atmospheric waves. As the cloud-train moves downwind from the island it spreads like a ship's wake for several hundred kilometres before blending in with the banks of cumuliform cloud to the north. This image was captured on December 19, 2005 by the Moderate Resolution Imaging Spectroradiometer (MODIS) device on board NASA's Terra research satellite.

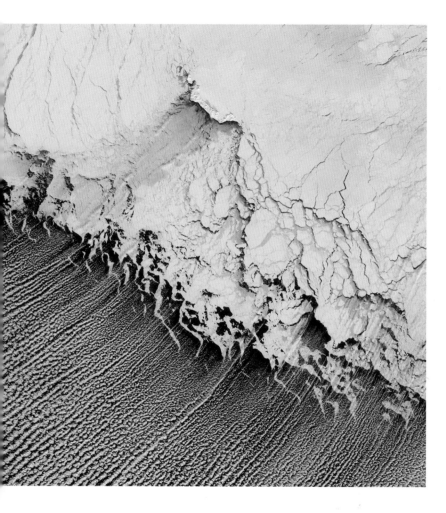

Alaskan cloud streets

Rows of small cumulus clouds stream out from the western edge of the sea ice over the Bering Sea near St Matthew Island, an isolated outpost of Alaska some 320km (200miles) offshore. Cloud streets are formed when a layer of cold air passes over a relatively warm surface – in this case the open water of the Bering Sea. As the cold, gusting air begins to rise, a stable layer of air above puts a cap on the convection causing the turbulent air to rise and sink in a low-lying vortex pattern as it continues its forward progression. Where the air rises, rolls of cumuliform clouds appear running parallel to the wind, but where the air sinks it remains clear of cloud. The result is a series of long, parallel lanes of cloud known as streets. This picture was taken on January 20, 2006 from NASA's Terra satellite.

Thundercloud from space

The sun throws long shadows across a vast Pacific cloudscape in which the anvil of a towering thundercloud can be seen centre left. Its summit has flattened out beneath the tropopause, a natural temperature inversion encountered at heights of around 15km (9miles) above the Earth's surface. Thunderclouds form when warm, moist air (which exists in abundance over tropical oceans) rises rapidly through solar convection, cooling to condense its payload of vapour into cloud. The process of condensation releases large amounts of latent heat energy which adds to the turbulence inside the clouds, where rapid growth can form updraughts of over 150kph (90mph). A modest storm cloud will contain more energy than any atomic bomb on Earth. This photograph was taken from the International Space Station on July 21, 2003, from an altitude of around 380km (240miles).

Dust and vortex clouds

As a windblown veil of dust and smoke approaches the Cape Verde islands from Africa's northwest coast, low-level breezes create a complex pattern of cloud streets and vortices that stream downwind from the islands. The term 'streets' refers to cumulus clouds lined up by the wind in parallel bands (as on page17), while 'vortices' refers to the wake patterns formed when the winds manoeuvre around the islands.

At the bottom left of the image is a bank of closed cell clouds which tend to occur in roughly hexagonal arrays in layers of air that have begun to convect due to heating from below and cooling from above. In closed cell formations warm air rises in the centres and sinks back around the edges of the clouds, forming a characteristic honeycomb pattern. This true-colour Terra MODIS satellite image was captured in 2003.

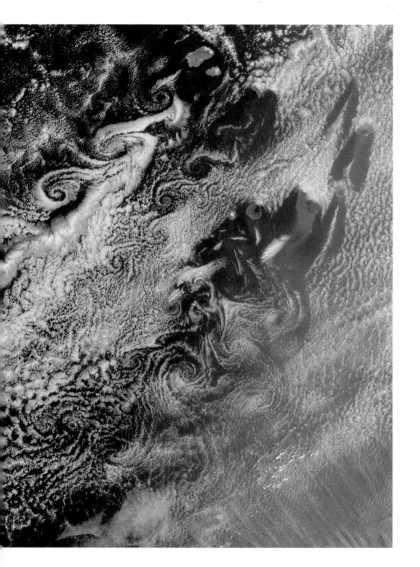

Von Kármán vortices over Cape Verde

Winds moving west over the archipelegic Cape Verde islands are disturbed by their passage over the high volcanic peaks, causing distinctive swirling eddies to form in their wake. These eddies – known as Von Kármán vortices (after the Hungarian physicist who first described them) – require wind speeds of 5–13m (16–42ft) per second, as well as a low-level temperature inversion (when the temperature of the air increases with altitude rather than decreases) in order to form. They tend to rotate in alternate directions over hundreds of kilometres, creating a characteristic paisley pattern that is rendered visible from the upper atmosphere by the clouds that form within them. This true-colour image – taken by NASA's Terra MODIS satellite – was captured on April 26, 2004.

Jungle in the clouds

A swirling layer of stratus nebulosus cloud is pierced by giant, spectral trees near the base of Mount Batur, Bali. Such cloud-wreathed jungles are not an unusual sight in equatorial regions where the air remains humid all year round. Roger Coulam – who took this atmospheric photograph on June 30, 2000 – recalls scrambling up the hillside before dawn, surrounded by hot boulders and steaming sulphur vents (Mount Batur being one of Indonesia's many active volcanoes): 'Resting near the summit as the sun came up, I looked down to see these ancient jungle trees breaking through the low-level cloud and mists.'

Jetstream cirrus over Egypt

Jetstreams are high-altitude, fast-moving air currents that flow through the tropopause some 7.6–10.6km (25,000–35,000ft) above the surface of the Earth. They are caused by extreme temperature differences in the upper atmosphere along the boundaries between polar and tropical air masses and can meander for thousands of kilometres at speeds of up to 640kph (400mph). Jetstreams are usually invisible but sometimes a tell-tale ribbon of cirrus cloud forms within the perimeters of the current, as can be seen in this impressive example observed by the crew of the Gemini 12 spaceship as they passed over Egypt in November 1966. In the foreground lies a wide expanse of red-tinted desert bisected by the River Nile, while the background is dominated by the distinctive outlines of the Red Sea and the Sinai Peninsula.

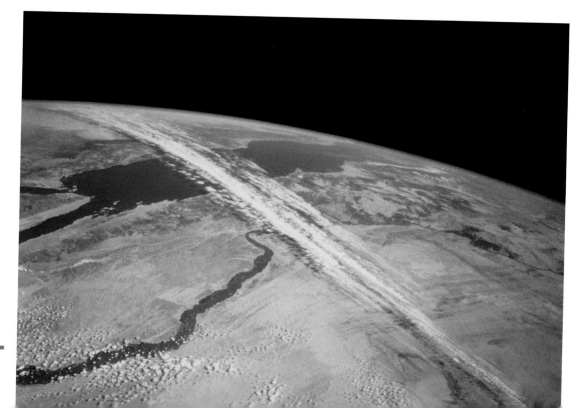

Clouds over the Pacific

An extensive layer of stratocumulus cloud hangs low over the Pacific Ocean, just over a 1km (3,289ft) above the surface. The picture was taken some 260km (160miles) above the Earth by the crew of the Apollo 17 space mission in December 1972. From this distance the breaks in the cloudbank where convection is slightly weaker resemble cracks in winter sea ice which, along with the line of cumulus outriders (top right of image), makes this extraordinary photograph look more like an aerial view of the Antarctic Peninsula than of a blanket of non-precipitating cumuliform cloud shrouding the warm Pacific.

Von Kármán vortex clouds

This image, captured by NASA's Terra satellite in January 2005, shows a single von Kármán vortex pattern flowing downwind from Heard Island, a sub-Antarctic volcanic peak in the southern Indian Ocean that is buffeted year round by the winds of the Furious Fifties (so called becasue of the 50 degree latitude south location). The uninhabited island has been a territory of Australia since 1947 and a UNESCO World Heritage Site since 1997.

Von Kármán vortices form when a fast-moving current of air flows around an obstacle in its path, creating spiralling eddies in its wake (see page 21). The dark colouration of the clouds in this image has been caused by the process of accumulation, where water droplets within the clouds merge with others to form larger droplets. Because the spaces between the droplets grow correspondingly wider, more light is absorbed within the clouds causing them to appear much darker than usual.

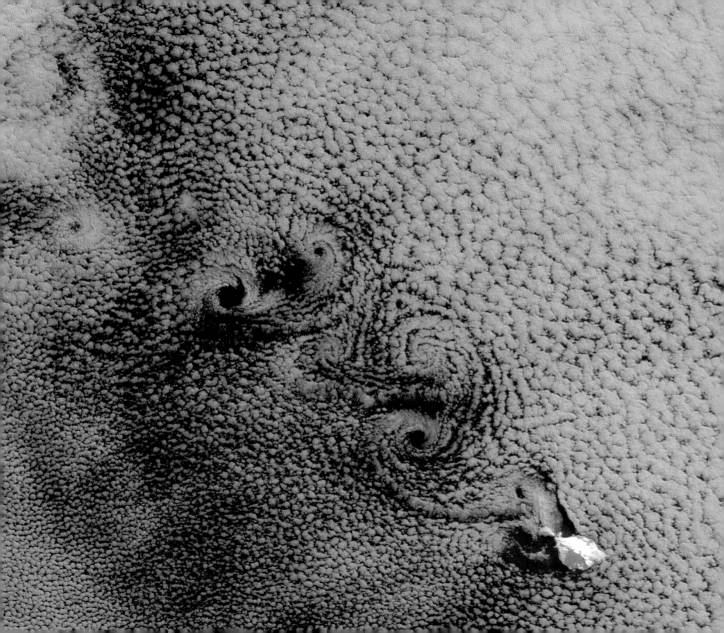

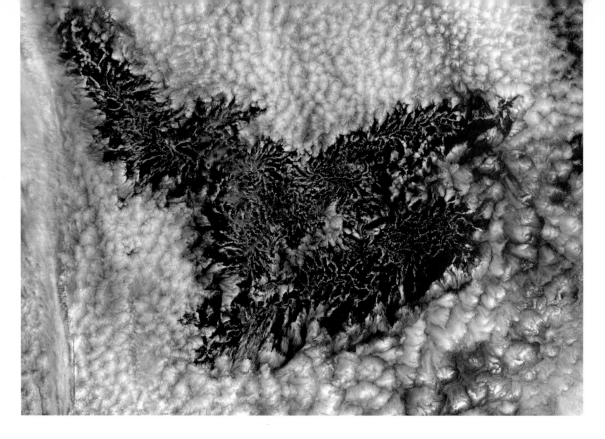

Open- and closed-cell stratocumulus clouds

Two distinct kinds of convection create two distinct arrays of marine stratocumulus cloud – open-cell and closed-cell – as can be seen in this Terra MODIS satellite image captured off the coast of California on August 16, 2002. Open-cell formations occur when cold air sinks in the centre of the cloud and rises at the edges, creating lacy, hollow-looking patterns such as those at the centre of the image. In contrast, the hexagonal closed-cell clouds around the perimeter have been formed by the reverse process, when warm air rises rapidly in the centres and cold air sinks around the edges, creating a characteristic honeycomb pattern that can also be seen in the image on page 20.

Backlit cap cloud

A layer of flattened cloud known as pileus (from the Latin for 'cap') can appear to hover above a growing cumulonimbus cloud, as in this beautifully backlit example photographed over the Maldive Islands. Pileus is formed when a layer of moist air is pushed up over the cloud's main summit, where it rapidly condenses into a supplementary cloud formed from supercooled water droplets (which remain liquid well below freezing temperature). The effect is usually short-lived with the cumulonimbus continuing to grow through convection, penetrating the pileus layer and absorbing it into cloud mass.

Fallstreak holes from above

Lit from below by the setting sun, a wide expanse of altocumulus cloud has what appears to be a lake of lava bubbling away at its centre. This 'lake' is in fact a fallstreak hole created by the sudden freezing of an isolated patch of supercooled cloud, which then falls away in a shower of ice crystals leaving a visible gap behind. ('Supercooled' clouds are composed of water droplets that remain in a liquid state at temperatures well below freezing.) Further photographs of the same phenomenon as seen from below are on pages 100 and 101, but this unusual panoramic shot shows an elongated fallstreak hole from just a few kilometres above it. The picture was taken by Marco Lillini, a commercial airline pilot from Italy who 'likes to photograph the view from his office window.'

Inside Hurricane Katrina

On August 23, 2005 a tropical depression began to form over the southeastern Bahamas. By the following morning it had developed into a hurricane and had been given a name: Katrina. It first made landfall near Miami as a Category One hurricane, with sustained wind speeds of around 120kph (75mph), but after it veered south into the Gulf of Mexico it intensified to a Category Five, with wind speeds of around 280kph (175mph). This photograph from inside Katrina's eyewall was taken from a WP-3D Orion research plane on the afternoon of August 28, when the hurricane was still out at sea. The National Oceanic and Atmospheric Administration (NOAA) routinely send research planes into hurricanes to collect vital information that will help determine their likely strength and direction. The billowing eyewall – the area around the hurricane's central 'eye' – is where the strongest winds are found, which were in excess of 250kph (150mph) when this extraordinary photograph was taken.

When Katrina made landfall again on the morning of August 29, 2005, she went on to cause tremendous damage throughout the state of Louisiana, breaching the levees around New Orleans in more than 50 places. By the end of the following day, when the hurricane finally dissipated, she had claimed nearly 2,000 lives and cost more than $50 billion in insurance claims. Katrina remains the most expensive hurricane in history.

Strange Shapes

Clouds come in a wide variety of distinctive shapes – from parallel lines to chaotic swirls – and some of them can be very strange indeed . . .

Mammatus at the base of a storm cloud

Usually appearing on the underside of an extended cumulonimbus anvil, mammatus clouds (from the Latin for 'udders') are associated with unstable, often stormy weather, though they can also be seen in relatively calm conditions, long after bad weather has passed. Their appearance is the result of pockets of cold, saturated air sinking rapidly from the top of a storm cloud, forming downward bulges or ripples at the base – an unusual example of clouds forming from convection in reverse (most cumuliform clouds being the result of pockets of warm air rising). Their shapes can vary considerably from long, undulating ripples covering many square kilometres, to smaller patches of near-spherical pouches, as in this somewhat menacing display of globular mammatus contorting itself over a college sports stadium in Hastings, Nebraska in June 2004.

Decaying altocumulus clouds

Like an aerial archipelago of floating islands, these isolated altocumulus cloudlets are fast giving up their contents in the form of virga – a term referring to any kind of precipitation that fails to reach the ground, evaporating back into the surrounding air instead. These rapidly diminishing cloudlets are likely to have been the patchy remnants of an earlier bank of altocumulus castellanus, broken up by an episode of atmospheric instability before descending to join the ranks of cumulus clouds below. These lower clouds have been arranged into neat parallel rows by winds blowing nearer the surface. This photograph was taken by commercial airline pilot Jurgen Oste.

Swirling cirrocumulus

An unusually-shaped cluster of cirrocumulus cloudlets dancing in the Alpine air above Vicosoprano, Switzerland. Cirrocumulus are among the rarest of all cloud types, forming high in the atmosphere from a mixture of ice crystals and supercooled water droplets. They form when turbulent convective currents encounter high cirrus or cirrostratus clouds, converting some of their ice crystals into supercooled droplets and breaking them down into grainy ripples of cloud, as can be seen in this striking image photographed in the Bergell Valley. Due to the unstable conditions in which they form, cirrocumulus cloudlets tend to be short-lived, either thinning out into veils of cirrostratus or joining up with neighbouring clouds to form a shallow, continuous formation across the sky. Broad, rippled displays of cirrocumulus stratiformis are often referred to as a 'mackerel sky' – and are a harbinger of stormy weather to come.

Pink UFOs

A stack of altocumulus lenticularis clouds hovers over the Alpujarra Mountains in southern Spain, stained by the rays of the setting sun. Lenticular clouds (Latin for 'lens-shaped') are a common sight in mountainous regions and are created when a stable layer of humid air is forced to rise over high ground, condensing its moisture into cloud. If alternate layers of moist and dry air are present the clouds will form in a vertical stack. As the airstream returns to its original level once it has passed over the obstacle, it sets up a standing wave effect on the lee side of the mountain. They have often been mistaken for UFOs.

Fluffy pink lenticular cloud

Another example of a lenticular cloud formation over the Alpujarra Mountains in southern Spain, this time brought about by a single layer of humid air rising and falling over a high obstacle to create a solitary line of almond-shaped wave clouds. Lenticular clouds have a typically dense and opaque appearance, being formed from large numbers of very small water droplets. Because they form within stable air flows they are often smooth in texture, although the slightly ruffled underside of this sun-raked example suggests a degree of instability in the airstream.

Lenticulars over Mount McKinley

Looking like clay on a potter's wheel, a striking pair of lenticular cloud formations shroud the twin summits of Mount McKinley, North America's highest mountain. Known as *une pile d'assiettes* (from the French for 'a stack of plates'), this arrangement is caused by alternate layers of dry and humid air flowing up over the Alaskan mountain from the northeast Pacific. As the air rises to cross the 6,194m (20,320ft) peaks its moisture condenses into distinctive layers of stationary cloud. McKinley is home to the world's second highest weather station, maintained at 5,800m (19,000ft).

Swirling lenticular cloud

A dramatic display of altocumulus lenticularis rears over the rugged mountains of South Georgia, a remote island group in the south Atlantic some 1,400km (864miles) southeast of the Falkland Islands. These beautiful undulating wave clouds can appear in strange and unexpected formations according to the movements of individual air currents downwind from intervening hill slopes – sometimes they resemble UFOs (as on the page 40) and sometimes they appear wild and monstrous, as in this unsettling example photographed from the British Antarctic Survey (BAS) research station at Bird Island.

Cirrus fibratus

Delicate white filaments of cirrus fibratus cloud dance high in the deep blue sky above the Corrieshalloch Gorge, a river canyon near Ullapool in the Scottish Highlands. Such fair weather clouds generally form when a layer of relatively dry air ascends to the upper troposphere at altitudes well over 6km (c. 20,000ft). When the air layer meets the subzero dewpoint the small amount of vapour it contains sublimes into ice crystals – sublimation being the process of changing directly from a gas to a solid, with no intermediate liquid state. These small icy cloudlets tend to appear on their own in cold, dry skies. If there was any more moisture around then other, thicker clouds would form at lower levels.

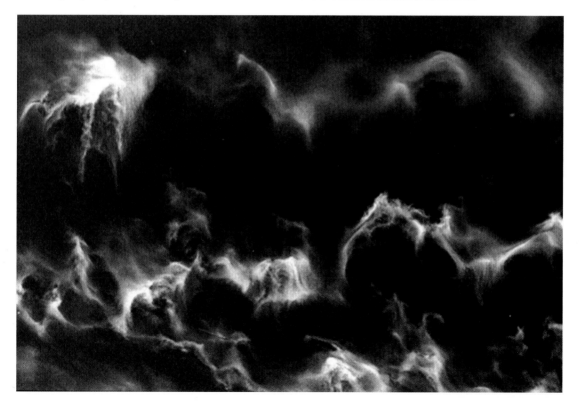

Roll cloud, Western Australia

A roll cloud is a horizontal, tubular formation that forms in the cold downdraughts that spread out ahead of an approaching storm (or, less commonly, at the tail end of a decaying storm). The rapidly sinking air mass can hit the surface so hard that it sends a wave of air gusting some distance away from the storm cloud itself. This cold flowing air will then slide underneath a layer of warmer air being drawn into the storm's vertical updraught, and as it does so it condenses the warm air's vapour into cloud. The resulting roll cloud is completely detached from the main storm cloud and can often be several kilometres long, as is the case with this impressive example seen heading inland over Shark Bay, Western Australia.

Dust devil

Like a cobra rising from a snake-charmer's basket, a dust devil dances in the air near Walsenburg, Colorado, USA. Dust devils are formed in updraughts of air from localized heating in dry conditions, and begin to whirl when the wind is funnelled through some kind of constriction, or because of differences in the roughness of the ground. They can grow quite large and vigorous, but this example, photographed by Roger Coulam during a storm chase in May 2003, is of the gentle, short-lived variety. Roger recalls how he had just pulled into a remote gas station when the dust devil appeared: 'I reached inside the van to grab my camera bag, spilling the expensive contents all over the floor. I grabbed one shot and it was gone, just as quickly as it started. My camera still bears the scars of the four foot drop to this day.'

Ring contrail

This circular condensation trail was left behind by a military aircraft on manoeuvres over Durham, England. It has begun to break up and merge with the high (6–12km/20,000–40,000ft)) cirrocumulus cloudlets already present in the atmosphere. Such contrails have done much to fuel the so-called 'chemtrail' conspiracy theory, which maintains that unusual sky tracks are the result of chemical or biological agents released at high altitudes during secret government experiments. Websites devoted to the conspiracy offer a range of imagined motives behind them – from biological weapons testing to human population control. Of course these claims have been refuted by the military as well as by federal agencies such as NASA, which leaves the conspiracy theorists even more convinced of the existence of a high-level cover-up.

Cap cloud on Mount Ararat

A shepherd stands gazing at a cap cloud shrouding the peak of Mount Ararat (the dormant volcano in northeast Turkey where Noah's Ark is reputed to have made landfall after the flood). Cap clouds are orographic clouds – they are formed by mountain slopes – and appear when moist air is forced up over a high obstacle by the wind. As the rising air cools its moisture condenses into a flat layer of cloud which then dissipates on the leeward side of the hill as the air begins to descend. With an elevation of more than 5,000m (nearly 17,000ft), Ararat intrudes deep into the cloud layer and is often seen wearing its distinctive stratiform cloud-hat.

Cirrus castellanus clouds

A collection of turretted cirrus castellanus cloudlets trail icy tendrils high in the sky over southwest Idaho, USA. These tendrils form when the slowly descending cloudlets encounter a deep layer of cold air that is moving at a stable speed, causing them to be spread across the sky – sometimes for considerable distances. Because these high, icy cirrus clouds spend their careers falling slowly through the sky they are classed as 'precipitating clouds', though they rarely produce anything other than trails of virga – short-lived streaks of ice and snow that evaporate long before reaching the ground.

Angels on horseback

Windblown trails of cirrus uncinus cloud, sometimes known as 'stringers' or 'mares' tails', are sculpted into dramatic shapes that appear to race across the upper atmosphere. Cirrus is a high-altitude (6–12km/20,000–40,000ft) ice crystal cloud which often appears wispy and diffuse compared to the majority of low and medium-level clouds – this is due to the low concentrations of ice crystals within the cloud compared to the high droplet concentrations in liquid water clouds. Like cirrus castellanus (opposite), this variety of cirrus is typically associated with calm conditions, though if it thickens and spreads (see page 96), it can be an indication that stormy weather is on its way.

Hawaiian UFO

A lenticular cloud hovers over Mauna Kea, the highest (and only snow-capped) peak in Hawaii. Lenticular clouds are formed when a layer of moist air rises as it encounters a high obstacle and sinks once it has passed it, creating a standing wave effect in the lee of the slope where moisture condenses to form what appears to be a 'hovering' cloud. In common with most apparently stationary lenticular clouds, this fine example hangs at a slight incline due to the downward flow of the leeside air, which only serves to enhance its resemblance to a classic UFO – a sight spooky enough to have stopped a skier in his tracks.

Kelvin-Helmholtz waves

Wave clouds typically form in stable conditions when wind speed and direction are both steady. But if strong horizontal winds disturb the boundary between a warm air mass and a layer of cooler air below, the upper layer may start to move at a faster rate than the lower, causing the 'crests' of the waves to advance ahead of the main body of cloud. The result is a rare, short-lived sequence of distinctive billowing formations known as a Kelvin-Helmholtz ('K-H') wave, after the 19th-century scientists who studied their motions. This example was photographed at Laramie, Wyoming (USA).

Altocumulus undulatus

Consisting of parallel bands of low to mid-level cumuliform cloud, this distinctive formation occurs when a layer of altocumulus cloud is affected by wind shear (when wind speed or direction changes abruptly with height), with the bands of cloud neatly arranged in the direction of the shear. Thickening bands of altocumulus are a reliable sign of an approaching warm front, with wet or stormy weather to come within the next 24 hours. This example was photographed in the Abruzzo National Park in central Italy.

New Zealand lennie stack

Like a visible cross-section of the lower atmosphere, a multi-layered stack of altocumulus lenticularis (or 'lennies') towers over Mount Ruapehu, an active volcano on New Zealand's North Island. This colossal cloud stack is created by a series of moist air layers lifted by the mountain. The cloud stack soars upwards from Ruapehu's eastern flank some 2,500m (8,000ft) in elevation, right up into the domain of the cirriform clouds, 6km (20,000ft) or so into the troposphere, where the tops of the clouds have begun to glaciate into wispy filaments of ice.

Orographic altocumulus

Airflows are typically more horizontal than vertical but sometimes when winds flow off an intervening hillside, strong vertical oscillations occur as the air attempts to stabilize. If the air at the top of these oscillations is stratified in terms of moisture content, clouds will form within the saturated layers. The result of this will be a lenticular cloud with a strongly layered appearance, such as the one seen in this photograph, a strangely sculptural example standing sentinel over a hillside as the sun begins to set. Persistent wave motions in the airflow can also lead to long chains of lenticular clouds extending far from the originating obstacle.

Cirrus plumes

A spreading band of cirrus spissatus cloud looms above a row of trees in the vanguard of an approaching warm front. Cirrus spissatus is a thickened variety of cirrus cloud which forms high in the troposphere (at altitudes of around 6–8km (c. 20,000–26,000ft). While most cirriform clouds remain thin and wispy (due to the relative sparseness of moisture in the upper air), this variety is fuelled by the incoming moisture that arrives in advance of the frontal system and can sometimes grow to cover much of the sky. If it does so, fetch an umbrella because wet and stormy weather could be on its way!

Optical Effects

Clouds are nature's kaleidoscopes, refracting and diffracting sunlight into vivid displays of colour. This section is devoted to the most beautiful of these cloud-induced light effects, from the pastel shades of iridescence to the bright flames of sun pillars and crepuscular rays.

Golden corona

Coronae are coloured rings or sequences of rings that appear around the sun or moon, filtered through thin layers of low or medium-level cloud. Lunar coronae are easier to see than solar varieties due to the glare of direct sunlight, but this striking example of a solar corona occurred soon enough after dawn to be visible through the burnished patch of altocumulus cloud, although the violet-blue inner aureole usual with solar coronae has been lit out leaving only the wider yellow-red outer bands visible. The phenomenon is caused by the diffraction (bending) of light by evenly sized water droplets or ice crystals within the cloud – the smaller and more uniform the droplets, the larger and brighter the corona's rings. Where the cloud droplets vary in size the radius of the rings also varies around their circumferences, as can be seen in this fine example of an early morning light show.

Glory from the air

A glory is an optical phenomenon produced by light scattered back towards its source by a cloud of uniformly sized water droplets. The diffracted light forms a sequence of coloured rings in the same chromatic order as those of the corona (see page 65), though they appear around the antisolar (or antilunar) point rather than directly around the sun or moon. Glories are often seen by mountaineers once they have ascended into the cloud layer, but they are more easily glimpsed from aircraft windows when passing over mist or cloud. This example was spotted on an afternoon flight between Oslo and Copenhagen in May 2007, shows the aircraft's faint shadow cast on to a thick bank of stratocumulus, surrounded by a radiating sequence of rainbow-coloured rings. The glory is so named because of the magestic effect it imparts, an effect known in China as 'Buddha's Light', the sight of which is regarded as auspicious.

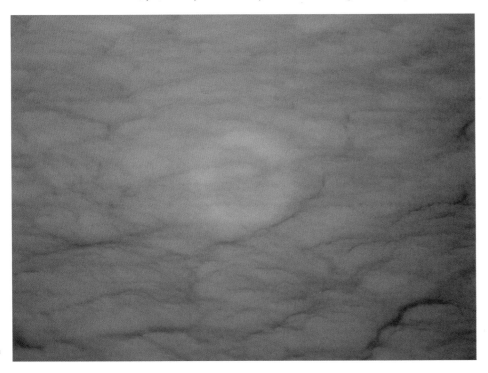

Rainbow with hail shower

A bright section of rainbow pierces a vigorous hail shower over the village of Pilsley, Derbyshire, England. Hail forms when warm updraughts of air send falling ice pellets back into the frozen centre of the cloud. The pellets grow through collision and freezing until they are too heavy to stay aloft, at which point they fall to the ground as hail. The bright sunlight that powered the hailstorm's convective updraughts also created the truncated arc of rainbow that descends from the cloud base. Rainbows are caused by water droplets dispersing sunlight into the colours of the visible spectrum. White light is refracted as it enters the droplets and then reflected off their back surfaces, being re-refracted on the way out at a range of optical angles. The order of the colours on a primary bow always begins with red on the outer edge: see page 70 for an example of a secondary (double) bow.

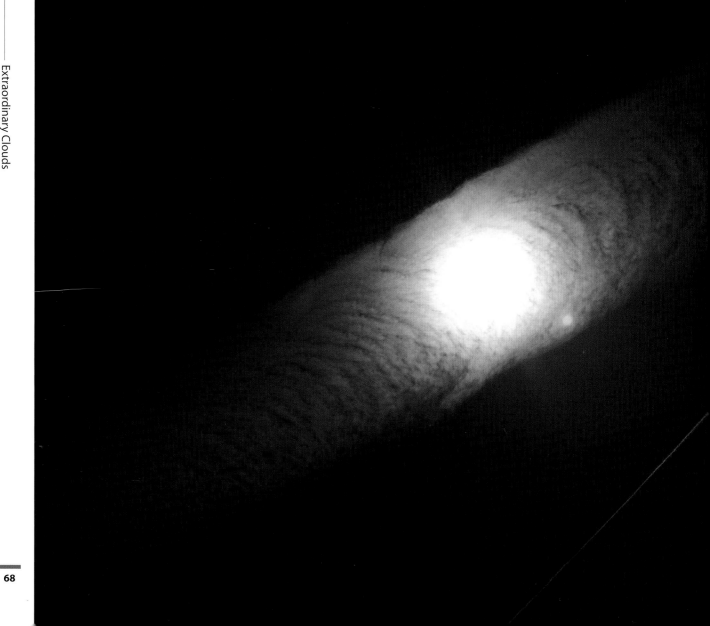

Swiss watch contrail

An aircraft contrail spreads across the afternoon sky, filtering the sun to create the striking impression of an oversized wrist watch hanging overhead. Contrails are prolific man-made clouds and are formed from the water vapour ejected from aircraft exhausts, usually at altitudes above 8km (26,000ft), where the air is extremely cold (less than -40°C/-40°F). Like natural cirrus clouds, contrails are mainly composed of slowly falling ice crystals, which can persist and spread over enormous distances depending on the prevailing winds, as well as on the amount of moisture already present in atmosphere. These conditions vary greatly with altitude, as can be seen from the second, higher contrail in the picture which has lingered in the sky without spreading. The photograph was taken from the Royal Horticultural Society's garden at Wisley, Surrey, England.

Double rainbow

Rainbows can only be seen when the sun is directly behind the observer and the airborne water droplets which refract the light are falling directly in front. Primary bows with a 42° radius are the most commonly seen variety (see page 67), but sometimes a larger secondary bow (of 52° radius) appears above the primary bow, as in this striking example of a double bow illuminating a rain cloud in Utah, USA. While the order of colours in the primary bow remains red on the outside, violet on the inside, the order is always reversed in the secondary bow. The dark area between the two bows is known as Alexander's band after Alexander of Aphrodisias, the 2nd century-Greek scholar who first described the phenomenon. It is caused by the deviation of light between the primary and secondary bows, darkening the sky between them. Three bows can be seen on rare occasions, depending on brightness and the human eye's ability to see it because the colours can be inverted.

Iridescent pileus

The supplementary feature known as 'pileus' forms above vigorous cumulus congestus or cumulonimbus clouds when a layer of moist air is suddenly forced up, causing renewed condensation above the main body of cloud. It is usually indicative of severe weather to come since it is formed by strong updraughts within a growing, unstable cloud. The flattened pileus often appears striated, as in this dramatically lit example photographed from an aeroplane over Sarawak, Borneo. The main convective cloud mass is in deep shadow while the backlit pileus is bright with iridescence.

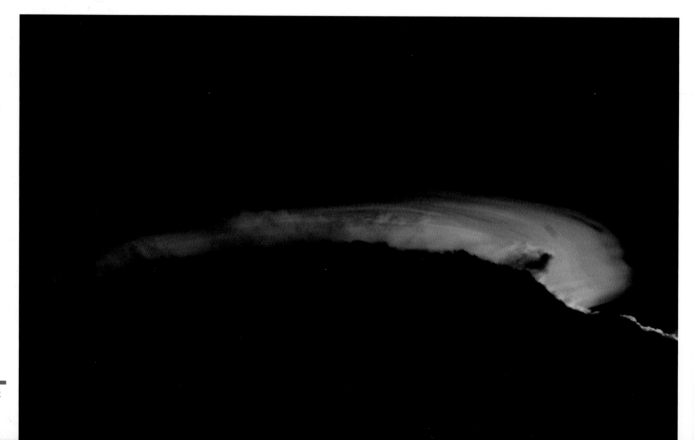

Fallstreak hole with circumzenithal arc

Fallstreak holes are created by the sudden freezing of an isolated patch of supercooled cloud, which falls away to leave a visible gap behind. In this example observed over Royston Heath, Hertfordshire, England, some of the remaining ice crystals have refracted low sunlight to form the halo effect known as a circumzenithal arc (CZA) – a band of bright prismatic colours resembling a section of inverted rainbow. Because ice crystals refract sunlight more effectively than water droplets, the colours of a CZA arc – which run from blue nearest the zenith to red nearest the horizon – are often brighter and more intense than those of a rainbow.

Noctilucent clouds

Also known as polar mesospheric clouds, noctilucent clouds are the highest clouds in our atmosphere, forming on the fringes of space some 80km (50miles) or more above the surface of the Earth. They consist of ice particles seeded on microscopic nuclei, although the precise mechanism of their formation in the cold, dry conditions of the mesosphere is still a matter of debate. Noctilucent clouds (from the Latin for 'night-shining') are usually seen around midnight during the summer months in high latitudes (above 50° north or south), as in this unusual 'herring-pattern' example, photographed above a lake in Finland. Though rare, these clouds are beginning to be sighted more frequently and at ever lower latitudes for reasons that are not yet known, but which may turn out to be connected to the warming of Earth's lower atmosphere.

Iridescent cirrocumulus

Tiny particles (either ice crystals or supercooled water droplets) have diffracted sunlight into the bright spectrum of colours that illuminate the frozen edge of this cirrocumulus cloudlet. The effect – which often takes the form of distinct bands of colour running along the perimeter of a cloud – occurs when a thin layer of mid-to-high altitude cloud moves close to the sun. The colour bands indicate the parts of the cloud where the ice crystals or supercooled water droplets are evenly sized – the more regular their size and arrangement the purer the colours will be.

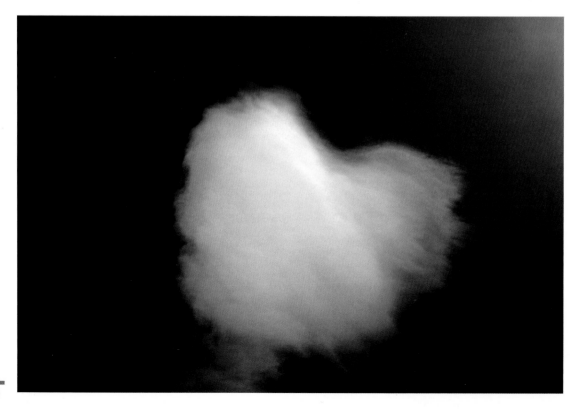

Blue sky halo

A halo is an optical phenomenon that appears near the sun or moon and is caused by the refraction of light through hexagonal ice crystals present in thin layers of cirriform cloud located in the upper troposphere, at altitudes of 6–10km (20,000–33,000ft). This example from Castle Rock, Colorado, USA, shows the arc of a partially formed solar halo refracted into bright rainbow colours by a patch of icy cirrostratus cloud. The colours run the opposite way to those of a rainbow, with blue on the outer edge shading towards red on the inner. The fragments of white cumulus cloud flanking the halo are much nearer to the ground than the high cirrostratus and reflect the light on what appears to be a sunny afternoon, though the appearance of a halo is sometimes a forewarning of approaching rain or snow.

Nacreous clouds

Nacreous ('mother of pearl') clouds, also known as polar stratospheric clouds, appear high in the atmosphere at 15–30km (10–20miles) above the Earth in latitudes higher than 50°, particularly in the northern hemisphere. They form in the freezing temperatures of the lower stratosphere, often below -80°C (-112°F), and are usually a mixture of nitric acid and ice crystals sourced from parcels of moist air that are forced up through the tropopause by the same orographic oscillations that are responsible for producing high lenticular wave clouds (such as those on page 95). The likeliest time to see nacreous clouds is during a winter sunrise or sunset when most of the sky is dark, leaving them lit by the sun from beneath the horizon. Their iridescent pastel colours can be magically beautiful – an effect heightened by their enormous distance from the viewer.

Irisation in altocumulus

Altocumulus is a mid-level cloud type composed of ice crystals or supercooled water droplets (or a mixture of the two), and so is well equipped to exhibit a wide range of optical phenomena, including irisation – the diffraction of light by uniformly sized particles within the cloud. The range of iridescent pastel colours is typical of the phenomenon which usually appears in bands along the thin edges of clouds as they pass over or near to the sun or moon.

Crepuscular rays

Crepuscular rays are beams of sunlight that are scattered and made visible by minute particles and compounds present in the lower atmosphere. They come in three distinct varieties: 1) the 'Jacob's Ladder' type that stream downwards from gaps in low cloud; 2) beams that rise and appear to diverge upwards from behind cumuliform clouds; 3) those that radiate from below the horizon, as in this fiery example in which the intense colouration is caused by the rays of the evening sun passing through layers of atmospheric haze. The vast rays emerge parallel to one another.

Alpine halo with sun dogs

Haloes are optical phenomena caused by the refraction of light through tiny hexagonal ice crystals. They often appear in conjunction with other optical effects such as sun dogs and parhelic circles, as in this fine example, photographed in the Austrian ski resort of Saalbach. In the centre a classic 22 degrees halo can be seen around the sun, intersected by an upper tangent arc, as well as by a pair of bright parhelia (also known as 'sun dogs') flanking either side. Parhelia (these are also caused by the refraction of light through horizontally aligned ice crystals) tend to appear when the sun is low in the sky, and will seem to move closer to the sun as it sets. Running through them is a faint line of light known as a parhelic circle, another refraction phenomenon that passes horizontally through the sun.

Lunar halo

Lunar haloes have the same origin as solar haloes (see page 82) – the refraction of light by hexagonal ice crystals suspended high in the troposphere in thin cirriform clouds (usually veils of cirrostratus). They tend to be seen more often than the solar variety due to the blinding glare around the sun during the day, and are safer to observe for the same reason. They typically occur within five days either side of a full moon; this fine 22 degrees example was photographed from the Atlas Mountains in Morocco where the sky was clear enough to show the red colouration on the halo's inner edge, shading towards blue on the outer edge (the reverse of the colour progression found in rainbows and coronae).

Sun pillar

A vertical shaft of light illuminates a layer of stratocumulus cloud above a calm evening sea: a sun pillar is an optical effect caused by light reflected from the horizontal surfaces of slowly falling, hexagonal ice crystals suspended in the atmosphere, typically in high cirrostratus clouds. Unlike refraction phenomena (such as the lunar halo, opposite) pillars are simply the collective glittering of millions of tiny ice crystals, so they reflect the colours of the rising or setting sun rather than dividing into the spectrum colours associated with refraction. They are usually only visible at sunrise or sunset, when the glare of the sun is least intense and can extend to more than 20° of arc above the horizon.

Iridescent cirrus cloud

Iridescence – streaks or patches of mother-of-pearl colouration – is usually associated with thin layers of mid to high-level cloud such as cirrus and cirrostratus, which form at altitudes above 6km (20,000ft) from ice crystals originating from the freezing of supercooled water droplets. The effect is caused by the diffraction of sunlight by evenly sized particles and often follows the shape of the cloud, with sinuous bands of colour forming where groups of ice crystals or supercooled droplets are of a uniform size and shape. The phenomenon is usually visible close to the sun, which is just out of shot at the top centre of the image.

Theatrical Skies

Great atmospheric dramas are in continuous production
all around the world, from the epic summer blockbusters
of supercell thunderstorms to the eerie displays of lenticular
clouds that rise above mountain scenery.

Silver ripples in the sky

One June morning brought an unusual sight to the residents of Cedar Rapids, Iowa, USA – an eerie rippling cloud formation hanging low over the city. In response to widespread concern the local television channel (KCRG-TV9) brought on their popular weatherman Joe Winters: 'We'll just call them wave clouds', Joe explained, 'the atmosphere always has waves in it, like the ocean. We just don't see waves often enough and today we had the opportunity to do that and it probably won't happen again for a long time.' This kind of low-hanging altostratus layer results from the lifting of large masses of humid air ahead of an incoming warm front, the rising moisture condensing into thick, undulating – and occasionally disconcerting – patterns of rippling cloud.

Supercell over Montana

A supercell is a severe thunderstorm with a deep rotating updraught (known as a mesocyclone) at its heart. Supercells are associated with strong winds, heavy rain, hail, lightning and destructive tornadoes, and can persist for many hours – although this dramatic example, photographed by the late Eric Nguyen, proved unusually short-lived. It passed over the Crow Indian Reservation in southeast Montana, USA, producing an occasional heavy burst of rain. Its high base resulted in rapid weakening and dissipation less than two hours after it first appeared.

Tornadic lightning strike

Lightning is a visible electrical discharge generated by powerful updraughts of air within large cumulonimbus clouds. Clusters of positive and negative charges become separated within the cloud, congregating in different regions – strong positive charges often build up at the top, while negative charges cluster at the base. When the potential difference between them becomes too great to bear, electrical energy is discharged in the form of lightning initiated by downward-moving leader strokes. What appear as single bolts of lightning are often sequences of near-instantaneous discharges that seek the ground in 'steps' – seen in this impressive shot of tornadic lightning in the American Midwest. The purple colouration of the air is due to the presence of rain in the atmosphere.

Lenticulars over Patagonia

A sky-filling display of altocumulus lenticularis soars over Lake Pehoe in
the Torres del Paine National Park in southern Chile. The region's complex
topography creates stable but multi-directional airflows, in which layers of
dry and humid air rise together, condensing their payloads of moisture into
strongly striated cloud formations. These formations can extend a great
distance over the snow-clad mountains and valleys of Magallanes Province.

Flailing cirrus

An early evening display of cirrus spissatus cloud, observed from the estuary of the River Fal near Devoran, England, one summer. This magnificent sky-filling display of cirrus persisted for 'several hours', as the photographer Stephen Burt recalls. The cloud originated from an approaching warm front that was beginning to lose forward momentum. Cirrus clouds are always worth keeping an eye on – if they stay much the same over a long period then the weather is likely to stay calm and fine, but if they begin to thicken and spread, dominating the sky, then bad weather will not be far away.

Wall cloud, Lincoln, Nebraska

A regular feature of supercell storm systems, wall clouds (sometimes known as pedestal clouds) are isolated lowerings attached to the storm cloud's rain-free base. They develop when rain-cooled air is pulled towards the mesocyclone (the supercell's violently rotating core), its moisture condensing at a lower level than the principal cloud structure itself. Wall clouds thus mark the area of strongest updraught within the storm, and are characterized by extremely strong winds – in fact tornadoes often form from within wall cloud structures, as seen on page 102.

Spectacular lenticular clouds

Vertical oscillations in the air flowing over the snow-clad mountains of South Georgia in the South Atlantic have produced dramatic swirls on the undersides of these lenticular clouds, creating a hauntingly sculptural effect in the dawn sky. The photographer – marine scientist Jamie Watts, who was based at the BAS research station on the island – recalls being woken by the early morning light: 'Through the windows was the most beautiful sky I have ever seen. I hurried to the end of the beach to get this photo. The young fur seals were neurotic and occasionally aggressive and, as I edged over the slippery rocks, I was right under the nose of a large, posturing adolescent.'

Fallstreak hole at sea

Fallstreak holes, which are also known as 'hole punch clouds', occur when patches of high cloud freeze and fall away as ice crystals, leaving visible gaps in the cloud layer. The cause of the phenomenon is not fully understood, though it seems to happen only in supercooled clouds – where water droplets remain in liquid form even at subzero temperatures. This extensive layer of altocumulus was punctured by a near-circular hole where only vestigial patches of icy cloud remain. Aircraft exhaust could play a part in the creation of hole punch clouds since supercooling occurs when there are not enough 'freezing nuclei' available for airborne water droplets to turn into ice. Since the microscopic particulates from aircraft exhaust are an abundant source of nuclei, could the fallstreak hole turn out to be yet another man-made phenomenon?

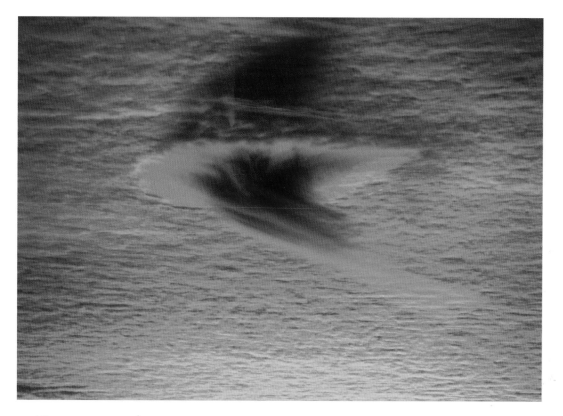

Fallstreak hole at sunset

This fallstreak hole has been captured in the process of jettisoning its icy contents into the evening sky over northwest Florida. The photographer, Vicki Harrison, recalls watching this glorious scene and marvelling at the way the streaks appeared to fall 'through' the hole. As seen in the lower half of the image, the falling ice does not get far before it begins to dissipate. If the atmospheric conditions are unfavourable to rain the ice crystals sublimate, changing state directly from a solid to a gas as they pass through a warmer layer of air, preventing it from reaching the ground.

Birth of a tornado

A tornado is a violent, rotating column of air that connects the base of a cumulonimbus storm cloud with the ground below. They form when powerful downdraughts drag the supercell's mesocyclone towards the ground, generating a visible condensation funnel that begins to throw up soil and debris as soon as it makes contact. This image, taken near Turkey, Texas, USA, shows the point at which this supercell thunderstorm became tornadic, the spinning updraught throwing out dust and soil as the funnel begins to form. The subsequent tornado tracked for some hours across the Caprock region of the Texas Panhandle, distributing powerful downbursts and gustnadoes in its wake.

Dust wave

Parmer County, Texas, USA – photographer Roger Coulam remembers it well: 'We watched as a huge storm developed and then suddenly sucked in too much cold air, collapsing and sending a wall of ferocious winds in our direction. It picked up enormous quantities of dust with gustnadoes spinning up in the towering, swirling red curtains in front of us. It hit at 60mph and we were forced to drive a couple of miles ahead of it, stopping for a minute or so to take pictures before it engulfed us again, filling the van with dirt and dust, tearing at the vehicle's doors.'

Gust front

A gust front is a leading edge of cold air that rushes downwards from a thunderstorm, spreading out fast when it hits the ground. They are often marked by turbulent shelf clouds, as in this example, photographed in Meade County, Kansas, USA. Roger Coulam recalls watching the gust front form and then suddenly break away from the storm: 'For a while we stood quietly with warm inflow winds on our backs, before running for cover as the icy blast of the wet outflow winds hit us in the face.' A violent hailstorm forced Roger and his fellow stormchasers to shelter beneath the canopy of a nearby gas station as nervous staff peered through the windows, alarmed at the arrival of the chasers.

The electrical sublime

Legendary storm photographer Eric Nguyen took this dramatic shot of a night-time supercell one June, after a long day of storm chasing across the east Colorado prairie, USA. 'What a way to end a perfect day!', he noted on his blog site. Two kinds of lightning – cloud-to-cloud (left) and cloud-to-ground (right) – flashed and growled beneath the silent canopy of stars, creating eerie beacons of intermittent light that were visible for many kilometres around.

Dust storm

This is another view of the severe tornadic supercell storm that features on page 102, and shows a later phase of its career when it was violently sucking in surrounding air, picking up large amounts of dust and soil, and sending out downbursts of up to 160kph (100mph). The photographer

Roger Coulam resorted to tying a chamois cloth over his camera in order to protect it from flying debris, as well as to provide an anchor to hold it down with both hands as the storm raged on. 'The lighting on this storm was unique', he says, 'and the noise of the monster unforgettable'.

Land of the long white cloud

New Zealand is nothing short of a lenticular cloud factory. The original Polynesian name for the island group was Aotearoa ('land of the long white cloud'), a name suggested by just this kind of formation seen massing above Mount Ruapehu, North Island. A familiar sight throughout New Zealand, 'lennies' are always localized phenomena and never spread far from their source. In stable wind conditions they can appear to 'hover' in one spot for many hours – the streams of moisture passing through the clouds, condensing at one end and evaporating out the other, like the disappearing ends of a conveyor belt.

Tornado and lightning in a Midwest field

A kilometre-wide wedge tornado sucks up several tonnes of reddish topsoil as lightning flies from the base of the parent cloud. What appears to be a single bolt of lightning is often revealed by the camera to be a sequence of near-instantaneous strokes that seek the ground in 'steps', as can be seen in this dramatic shot of a storm-battered wheatfield in the American Midwest. Mature wedge tornadoes such as this have a wider damage path than classic funnel-shaped 'twisters', and are often longer-lived, tracking over land for an hour or more and leaving a tremendous amount of damage in their wake. Tornadoes are graded from 0–5 on the Enhanced Fujita (EF) Scale (based on the amount of damage they cause) and from 0–11 on the TORRO Intensity Scale (based on their estimated wind speeds). This monster may well have been graded an EF Scale 4 or even 5.

Scorpion's tail tornado

For meteorologists the word 'tornado' refers to the entire vortex of wind that connects a supercell thunderstorm with the ground below. For the rest of us it means the visible funnel that descends from the base of a storm cloud – as in this dramatic example photographed by Roger Coulam in Clay County, Nebraska, USA. Cold outflow winds had nudged the funnel away from the main cloud base, creating a distinctive 'scorpion's tail' effect. Roger managed to take two shots of the powerful twister before a hailstone the size of a golf ball struck him on the head, at which point he decided to call it a day. The storm went on to generate at least a dozen further tornadoes including, at one point, three on the ground at the same time, escessive even for the American Midwest, (an area that experiences more than 1,000 tornadoes a year.

Dusty tornado

Tornadoes come in a variety of shapes and sizes with footprints ranging from 2–3km (1–2 miles) in diameter to only a couple of metres (less than 10ft). Pictured here is an this example of a small tornado kicking up dust near Northam, Western Australia. Tornadoes such as this tend to be short-lived, doing little in the way of damage (it would have registered as 0 on the EF Scale). Nevertheless they are an impressive sight as they track across the landscape, twisting and turning with the wind before eventually roping out and dissipating, leaving trails of scattered topsoil in their wake.

'A saucer-shaped supercell'

Stormchaser Jim Reed took this dramatic photograph after a prolonged pursuit of the isolated supercell as it raged across south-central Kansas, USA. A supercell is a severe, long-lived thunderstorm with a deep rotating updraught at its heart, the turbulent base of which can clearly be seen picking up debris and hurling it over the wheatfield. Jim Reed later recalled that the densely striated cell was 'one of the most unusually shaped storms that I had ever witnessed'. He had spent the afternoon following it as it made its way south – which was unusual in itself since most storms in the Midwest track northwards – and just as the sun was setting, he jumped from the vehicle, 'dodging hailstones the size of golf balls', to capture this stunning image of 'a rare, rain-free, isolated, saucer-shaped supercell backlit by the setting sun'.

Tornado in the Texas panhandle

The debris cloud at the base of a tornado's funnel will take on the colouration of whatever environment it happens to be in, from bright white (when passing over water or snow) to nearly black (when picking up a lot of loose dirt and debris). The base of this impressive 'elephant's trunk' tornado was stained reddish-brown by sand from the banks of the Red River, near Silverton, Texas, USA, over which it passed during its 40-minute career. Tornadoes generate some of the strongest winds on Earth, which can be in excess of 500kph (300mph), and Eric Nguyen, the photograph's creator, described how he was unable to stand up at times, even though the storm itself was almost a couple of kilometres (over a mile) away.

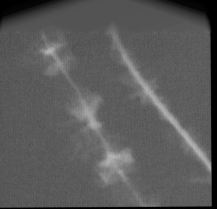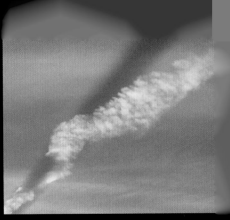

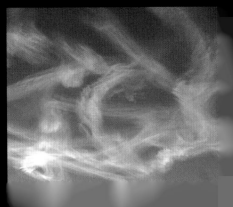

Man-made Clouds

The impact of human activity has made its mark on every corner of
our planet including the atmosphere, where man-made clouds
are fast becoming the most recognizable clouds in the sky.

Fumulus cloud

'Fumulus' is a variety of man-made cumulus cloud that forms above industrial cooling towers, in this case the eight chimneys of the Ratcliffe-on-Soar power station – a 2,000-MW coal-fired plant near Nottingham, England. The warm, moist air from the cooling towers rises and expands, condensing into a low-lying cumulus cloud, the base of which is only a few hundred metres (little more than a thousand feet) above the ground. If moisture is already present in the atmosphere fumulus clouds can grow to considerable sizes and drift for some distance across the surrounding area, but in this instance on a mild day with only a light breeze, the cloud remained *in situ* above the source rather than drifting downwind. The photographer Stephen Burt recalls taking this picture in 1981, while travelling down the M1 motorway!

Music sheet sky I

This photograph, taken only 90 minutes after the Swiss watch picture on page 69, shows a near-parallel sequence of spreading contrails from aircraft following closely aligned flight paths over southeast England. The looping patterns within the slowly sinking ice formations are caused by the trailing vortices left behind in the wake of the passing planes, while their progressive displacement and spreading is caused by strong winds and ambient moisture present in the upper troposphere. The coloured spots in the image are due to 'flare' (internal reflections in the camera's lens system) and were not a visible element of the cloudscape.

Noctilucent rocket trail

A short-lived nacreous noctilucent cloud formed from the contrail of a high-altitude missile launched from the White Sands Missile Range in New Mexico, USA. The vapour from the missile's exhaust has frozen in the cold upper atmosphere, where its ice crystals diffract sunlight from below the horizon into a brilliant display of noctilucence. The uppermost parts of the cloud appear iridescent, resembling polar stratospheric ('nacreous') clouds (see page 78), while the lower parts are redder due to the scattering of blue light by dust and water in the lower atmosphere. Its convoluted shape is due to the differing wind speeds encountered at different altitudes. The photograph was taken just before dawn from the appropriately named Superstition Mountains, east of Phoenix, Arizona.

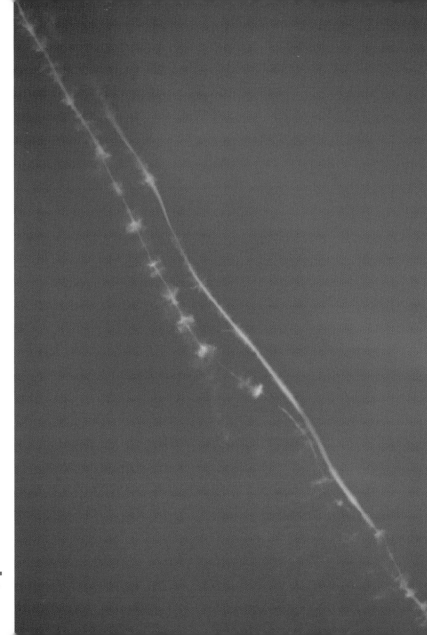

Barbed wire contrails

The exhaust from a twin-engine aircraft breaks
up into two distinctive-looking part-contrails,
indicating a rapid vertical and horizontal change
in atmospheric conditions at aircraft level,
some 8km (26,000ft) above the ground. Most
commercial airliners are equipped with either
two or four jet engines, but usually the resultant
contrail forms a single line that can either
dissipate or persist for several hours, depending
on the temperature, humidity and wind
conditions present in the upper troposphere.
These fast-evaporating examples suggest
that the blue sky over Berkshire, England, was
relatively moisture-free when Stephen Burt took
this photograph, 'looking almost vertically close
to the zenith, with a medium telephoto lens'.

Wing clouds

Gathering like foam on the wings of a Tornado fighter bomber, these curious artificial clouds are caused by the sudden drop in air pressure above an aircraft's wings as it pulls up into a high speed 'stall' (an effect enhanced by the Tornado's swing wings as they adjust for the drag effect introduced by the rapid reduction in thrust). The sudden drop in pressure forces the moisture immediately above the wings to condense into clouds, a short-lived phenomenon analogous to the sonic boom cloud on page139, although in this case the effect occurs at much lower speeds.

Contrail shadow

Low evening sunlight casts an upward shadow onto a layer of cirrostratus cloud above a variably spreading contrail over Dundee, Scotland. Its twisting shape creates a curious perspectival effect in which the contrail appears to have descended lower than it really has. As with the ring contrail on page 49, this kind of optical effect has helped perpetuate the so-called 'chemtrail' conspiracy theory, which maintains that certain uncharacteristic sky tracks have nothing to do with the vapour expelled from aircraft exhausts, but are caused instead by the systematic release of chemical or biological pathogens into the upper atmosphere by shadowy agents of the state.

Pyrocumulus cloud

Pyrocumulus is a cumuliform cloud produced by the intense heating of moisture-laden air by combustion occurring at ground level. Such clouds often appear above man-made sources of fire, but can also be generated naturally by erupting volcanoes or forest fires, growing large and vigorous enough to extinguish the flames that created them. Some can even grow powerful enough to produce lightning, generating more fires and fire clouds. This image was taken above a burning patch of forest in northwest Tasmania and has generated powerful hot air currents which – suffused with moisture from the burning vegetation – have risen rapidly, cooling and condensing their vapour into a large-scale cumuliform cloud.

Fumulus from high above

The cooling towers of Didcot power station in Oxfordshire, England, poke through a low blanket
of stratus clouds as billows of 'fumulus' from the combustion of coal and gas gather in the calm air
some 3km (10,000ft) above them. In contrast to the example of the same phenomenon seen on
page 120, the relative lack of moisture in the middle air means that the fumulus has neither persisted
nor merged into a large cumuliform structure, but instead has evaporated fairly quickly in the drier
layer above the stratus. A third layer of cloud can be seen higher in the sky, which appears to be a
thickening band of icy cirrostratus advancing over the western horizon ahead of an approaching front:
a sign that a period of unsettled weather is likely to be on its way.

Music sheet sky II

Riding high above an assortment of cumulus and altocumulus cloudlets is a near-parallel sequence of crenellated contrails from aircraft following the flight paths over the coast of Brittany, France. The increase in aviation over the past half century has transformed the contrail into the world's most abundant cloud type, though the long-term implications of this are far from understood. Data from the contrail-free skies that followed the 9/11 attacks (when all commercial flights in the USA were grounded for three days after the attacks) showed slightly warmer days and slightly cooler nights than usual, caused by additional sunlight reaching the ground by day and additional radiation escaping at night. Whether this means that contrails have an overall warming or cooling effect has yet to be established, but it is clear that these increasingly prolific man-made clouds exert a measurable influence on our atmosphere.

Propeller tip vortices

Vortices are tubes of circulating air that trail behind the wings and propellers of aircraft as a by-product of aerodynamic lift. The intense low pressure inside their spinning cores can encourage ambient water vapour to condense into droplets, causing short-lived loops of cloud to develop within them, rendering the trailing vortices briefly visible. In this example the four propellers of a Hercules aircraft flying low over the south of France appear garlanded with ribbons of cloud created in the airfoils' turbulent wake. Though such clouds usually extend for only a few metres (little more than ten feet) before evaporating into the surrounding air, the vortices themselves can grow surprisingly large and powerful, posing a serious hazard of viscous and turbulence effects for other aircraft flying nearby, particularly during take-off and landing.

Hovering pyrocumulus

Cooked up from the thermal currents above a burning field of stubble near Salisbury, England, a sooty pyrocumulus hovers eerily in the evening sky. Though on a much smaller scale than the forest fire example on page 127, the same processes are at work here – rising heat and moisture from the burning vegetation creates a warm and humid air mass, stoked with minute particles of smoke and ash. These particles act as condensation nuclei, on which the rising water vapour condenses into droplets (while encouraging ambient moisture to condense as well) to form a turbulent low-lying cloud. Unlike the extensive forest fire cloud, this one is likely to have proved short-lived. As soon as the stubble burning began to die down, the dark little fire-cloud would have started to decay, scattering its sooty contents over the field.

Contrails at sunset

Like wartime searchlights fanning the night sky, a fleet of icy contrails catches the last of the evening light. This photograph was taken at the end of an autumn day with strong northwesterly upper winds which caused the older contrails (left) to spread from right to left, creating an extensive bank of artificial cirrus cloud. Two younger contrails which are only just beginning to spread have formed a striking sunlit saltire at an altitude of about 12km (8miles) above the ground over Stratfield, Mortimer, in Berkshire, England. Their crenellated texture is caused by the trailing vortices left behind in the aircrafts' wake.

Space shuttle contrail

A twisted ribbon of icy contrail hangs over the coast of Florida following a launch of one of NASA's three remaining space shuttle orbiters. The shuttle's copious exhaust plumes – which are 97 per cent water – freeze in the upper atmosphere during the eight minutes it takes the craft to reach orbit in the thermosphere, more than 300km (190miles) above the Earth. The varying winds at different altitudes often sculpt the frozen contrails into sinuous shapes, as in this fine example photographed from the Banana River Bridge, 18km (12miles) south of the Kennedy Space Center, USA. The shuttle's long exhaust plumes have been known to trigger lightning by providing a current path to the ground, which is why no launch takes place if a cumulonimbus anvil cloud is present anywhere within a 16km (10 mile) radius of the launch site.

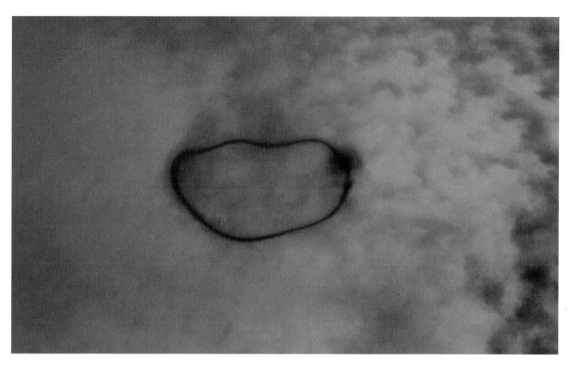

Here be dragons

A smoke ring hovers in the sky above an airfield in Scotland, blending in with the low base of a stratocumulus cloud. While not strictly a cloud or a contrail formation, it is nonetheless a striking atmospheric effect and one rarely caught on film. The photograph was taken by the meteorologist Norman Elkins at an airshow in Leuchars, Fife, Scotalnd. The weather was calm as an RAF jet simulated a low-level bombing run; as Norman recalls, 'the accompanying explosions generated this smoke ring along the length of which the thread was rotating rapidly about itself. One can only surmise that a vortex created by the passage of the aircraft had transformed the smoke into this ring and initiated the rotation in the calm environment.' A similar spectacle was photographed in July 2003 after a transformer was struck by lightning in San Antonio, Texas, USA, generating much consternation in the pages of the local press.

Sonic boom cloud

This rare image, taken by Ensign John Gay from the deck of the USS *Constellation*, shows the moment that an F/A-18 Hornet fighter jet breaks through the sound barrier over the Pacific Ocean, causing a short-lived sonic boom cloud to form. The science behind this unusual phenomenon has yet to be precisely established, but it seems to occur when a jet fighter accelerates at low altitudes over water, moving fast enough to cool the air around it. As the plane approaches the speed of sound over water (c. 1,200kph/750mph) the pressure created by the forward sound waves squeezes moisture in the air into a ball of cloud that grows rapidly over the moving aircraft. These man-made clouds last only a few seconds, but are, as Ensign Gay says, 'the coolest thing you have ever seen'.

Index

Picture Credits

Special thanks to Gavin Pretor-Pinney of the Cloud Appreciation Society and Steve Jebson of the National Meteorological Library and Archive for their help with finding the pictures and tracing copyright holders.

Cover image, 38 © Jurgen Oste; 12 © Stephen Cook; 13 © Sandy Boulter; 14 © Marco Cappelletti; 16, 20, 21, 28 © Jeff Schmaltz/NASA; 27 © Jacques Descloitres/NASA; 17 © Sciences DAAC; 18, 24, 25, 32, 44, 52, 53, 55, 57, 61, 75, 76, 78, 86, 110, 122, 138 © Science Photo Library; 23, 48, 97, 102, 104, 105, 108, 112 © Roger Coulam; 29, 74 © John Deed/www. flyingpigeon.com; 30 © Marco Lillini; 37 © Jorn Olsen; 39 © Heinz Bittner; 40 © Ian Dennis; 41 © Maria Carreras; 42, 51, 71, 92, 93, 94, 115, 116 © Corbis; 45 © J.M. Pottie; 46 © Jason Cutler; 49 © Dr R. Harris; 56 © Prof. A.H. Aver Jnr; 58 © J. Bowskill; 59 © P.D. Harris; 64, 66, 68, 96, 120, 121, 124,

135 © Stephen Burt; 67 © J.M. Moore; 72 © Randy Yit; 77 © Jim Karanik; 80 © Andrew David Kirk; 81, 113 © P J May; 83 © Thomas Dossler; 84 © A. Best; 85 © R.I. Lewis-Smith; 90 © Jane Wiggins; 98 © Jamie Watts; 100 © J.M. Attwell; 101 © Vicki Harrison; 107 © Eric Nguyen; 109 © Glyn Hubbard; 125 © Micahel Jacobssen courtesy of highgallery.com; 125 © Ken Bushe; 127 © Gary McArthur; 129 © David Fuller; 130 © Philippe Bouasse/Devarieux; 132 © I.M. Brown; 133 © G.J. Jenkins; 136 © Hanford R. Wright; 137 © N. Elkins.

These images have come from many sources and acknowledgment has been made wherever possible. If images have been used without due credit or acknowledgment, through no fault of our own, apologies are offered. If notified, the publisher will be pleased to rectify any errors or omissions in future editions.

Further Reading

Day, John A., *The Book of Clouds* (New York, 2006)

Dunlop, Storm, *Weather: Spectacular Images of the World's Extraordinary Climate* (London, 2006)

Hamblyn, Richard, *The Invention of Clouds: How an Amateur Meteorologist Forged the Language of the Skies* (London, 2001)

–, *The Cloud Book: How to Understand the Skies* (Newton Abbot, 2008)

Herd, Tim, *Kaleidoscope Sky* (New York, 2007)

Higgins, Gordon, *Weather World: Photographing the Global Spectacle* (Newton Abbot, 2007)

Hollingshead, Mike and Eric Nguyen, *Adventures in Tornado Alley: The Storm Chasers* (London, 2008)

King, Michael D., et al (eds), *Our Changing Planet: The View from Space* (Cambridge, 2007)

Met Office, *Cloud types for observers: reading the sky* (Exeter, 2006)

Pedgley, David E., 'Some thoughts on fallstreak holes', *Weather* 63 (2008): 356-60

Pretor-Pinney, Gavin, *The Cloudspotter's Guide* (London, 2006)

–, *A Pig with Six Legs, and Other Clouds that Look Like Things* (London, 2007)

Reed, Jim, *Storm Chaser: A Photographer's Journey* (New York, 2007)

Wilcox, Eric M., *Clouds* (London, 2008)

World Meteorological Organization, *International Cloud Atlas*, 2 vols (Geneva, 1975; 1987)

Acknowledgments

It is a pleasure to thank those who have helped during the process of researching *Extraordinary Clouds*, especially Neil Baber of David & Charles, Gavin Pretor-Pinney of the Cloud Appreciation Society, Martin John Callanan, artist in residence at the UCL Environment Institute, and Steve Jebson of the National Meteorological Library and Archive. A thousand thanks are also due to Stephen Burt and Roger Coulam, who provided essential background information to their own photographs, as well as insights into some of the others, and to Norman Elkins for explaining what was going on in his smoke ring photo (see page 137). And to the many other photographers (both amateur and professional) whose images are included here: thank you, and keep on looking up!